WOODWIND INSTRUMENTS

*Purchasing, Maintenance,
Troubleshooting,
and More*

CHARLES WEST

Published by
Meredith Music Publications
a division of G.W. Music, Inc.
1584 Estuary Trail, Delray Beach, Florida 33483
http://www.meredithmusic.com

MEREDITH MUSIC PUBLICATIONS and its stylized double M logo are trademarks of
MEREDITH MUSIC PUBLICATIONS, a division of G.W. Music, Inc.

Text and cover design: Shawn Girsberger

International Standard Book Number: 978-1-57463-145-6
Cataloging-in-Publication Data is on file with the Library of Congress.
Library of Congress Control Number: 2016912266
Printed and bound in U.S.A.

CONTENTS

Acknowledgements vi

Introduction vii

Woodwinds in General: Problems and Solutions
Applicable to All Woodwind Instruments 1

  Instrument Selection 1
  Maintenance and Storage 1
    Lubricants and Polishes 1
    Moisture Removal 2
    Temperature 3
    Assembly and Handling 3
  Troubleshooting 4
  Basic Woodwind Toolbox 8
  Tuning 9

Flute and Piccolo 11

  Purchasing 11
    Options 11
    Recommended student flute brands 12
    Step-up 12
  Maintenance and Storage 13
    Moisture Removal 13
    Lubricants and Polishes 14
    Storage 14
  Troubleshooting 14
    Pitch 15
    Response 16
    Mechanical 17

iii

Oboe and English Horn 18

Purchasing 18
Options 18
Recommended beginning and intermediate brands 18
Professional oboes 19

Maintenance and Storage 19
Moisture 19
Oiling keys 20
Temperature and humidity 20

Troubleshooting 21
Pitch 21
Response 23
Mechanical 25

English Horn 26
Purchasing 26
Other issues 26

Oboe and English Horn Reeds 27
Recommended Suppliers for Oboe Reeds 27

Clarinet 29

Purchasing 29
Recommended student clarinet brands 29
Step-up between beginning and professional instruments . . . 29

Maintenance and Storage 30

Troubleshooting 31
Pitch 32
Response and Annoying Noises 34
Mechanical 35

E-flat Clarinet 37

Bass Clarinet 37

Reeds 38

Mouthpieces 38

Ligatures 39

Barrel Joints 39

Saxophone 40

Purchasing 40
New saxophones 40
Older instruments 41

Mouthpieces 41
  Classical 41
  Jazz 41
Maintenance and Storage 42
Troubleshooting 44
  Pitch 44
  Response 45
  Reeds 46

Understanding Clarinet and Saxophone Reeds 47
  General Information 47
  Recommended Brands 47
  Reed Care, Break-in, Storage and Adjustment 48
  Understanding Reed Warpage 49
  Balance 50
    Testing for balance 50

Bassoon 52
  Purchasing 52
    Recommended student bassoons 52
    Step-up and professional 53
  Maintenance and Storage 53
  Troubleshooting 53
    Pitch 54
    Response 55
    Mechanical 56
  Bassoon Reeds 58
    Recommended Suppliers for Bassoon Reeds 58
    Problems with Bassoon Reeds 58
    General Reed Knowledge for the Non-Bassoonist 59

GLOSSARY 60

ABOUT THE AUTHOR 64

ACKNOWLEDGEMENTS

It has been my honor and pleasure to collaborate with my colleagues at Virginia Commonwealth University as contributing editors of each section. These are Tabatha Easley—flute, Alyssa McKeithen—oboe, Bruce Hammel—bassoon, and Albert Regni—saxophone. Each one of these professionals' contributions has strengthened and refined the advice and recommendations contained within.

Additional contributions include photographs by Robert Pratt and Susan Liu, graphics by Ze Huang, and design and layout by Shawn Girsberger. Thanks to the Jupiter and Miyazawa corporations for permission to use pictures and graphics.

Special thanks and highest praise to Garwood Whaley, who suggested the idea and whose advice and support have improved the final product at every turn along the way. And for her patience and support, not to mention the invaluable perspective gained through her years as an award-winning secondary school instrumental music teacher, my wife Mary Jo deserves my most sincere thanks.

cw

INTRODUCTION

I n a little over forty years of woodwind teaching, certain problems present themselves repeatedly. This handbook is almost autobiographical—an accumulation of problems and solutions, many of which have involved collaboration with some of the finest specialists in our profession.

This book attempts to assist you with selecting and purchasing equipment, maintenance, storage and troubleshooting—including pitch, response, mechanical and tonal issues—that arise in our teaching. All pedagogical references are to my WOODWIND METHODS: An Essential Resource for Conductors, Educators and Students, (ISBN 978-1-57463-436-5) also published by Meredith Music Publications.

My sincere hope is that the present book demystifies many of the problems you face as you navigate the complicated jungle of woodwind instruments, and makes a significant contribution to your success.

Anything worth doing is worth doing well!

WOODWINDS IN GENERAL: PROBLEMS AND SOLUTIONS APPLICABLE TO ALL WOODWIND INSTRUMENTS

Instrument Selection

The woodwind instrument you select should have the following qualities:

- It will make an appealing sound

- The scale will be even—some notes will not be muffled with others that are bright. (See the commentary included with the fingering charts in WOODWIND METHODS (ISBN 978-1-57463-436-5) for discussions of notes which are typically problematic on all five woodwinds.)

- The scale of the instrument will be true or nearly true to an electronic tuner. (Always take a tuner when buying an intermediate or professional instrument.)

- The tone focus and quality can be retained at both high and low dynamic levels.

- Other considerations such as resale value, repair record and serviceability may have an influence as well, especially for step-up and professional instruments.

- Always develop strong working relationships with local music stores, and purchase instruments from a reputable music dealer.

Maintenance and Storage

Lubricants and Polishes

- Use cork grease for cork tenons, bassoon bocals, and saxophone neck corks only, to lightly lubricate them for convenient assembly. Do not use cork grease on metal (flute) tenons or on string (bassoon)

1

tenons which are coated with paraffin. Do not use cork grease on an oboe reed staple, on cork pads or striker bumpers, or on flute headjoint corks.

- Oil the mechanism periodically to lubricate moving parts and to prevent rust on rods and pivot screws. Oilers made specifically for woodwind instruments are available, or apply a small drop of key oil or clean motor oil on the end of a toothpick to every hinge point where one piece of metal moves against another, and then wipe off the excess. A small amount of oil two or three times a year should be sufficient.

- Oiling the wood itself is a subject upon which there is considerable disagreement—some people never oil, and others do so regularly, especially in the Fall as the air becomes drier. Those who advocate oiling a wood instrument do so because oil is absorbed and lost by the instrument much more slowly than water, so the presence of the oil maintains a more-or-less constant moisture level. Commercial bore oil or sweet almond oil is used. Dedicate one chamois swab only to oiling: apply a few drops of oil to the swab, run it through the bore until you see the shine of the oil without dry streaks and then use the same swab to oil the outside of the instrument everywhere except where the oil might run onto the pads. Place the instrument in the case overnight and wipe off any excess oil in the morning. *Do not interchange key and bore oil— they are entirely different products.*

- Wood bassoons also need oil occasionally. Most technicians use either light mineral oil or linseed oil, and they remove all of the keywork from the instrument to protect the pads.

- *Never use commercial silver polish on a woodwind instrument.* because it contains an abrasive which can accelerate mechanism wear in an instrument. Chemically-treated polishing cloths may be purchased in a music store are effective and safe.

Moisture Removal

- Water should be removed from a woodwind instrument with an appropriate swab after playing and often intermittently while playing to keep the instrument clean and to avoid the accumulation of water in a single hole that causes a particular note to "gurgle." Do not store the damp swab inside the bore of the instrument.

- Remember that the water in a woodwind instrument is more condensation than saliva. So a cold instrument will accumulate considerable moisture until it becomes warm. The warmer the instrument, the less condensation, so, water is a greater problem in cold situations than in warm ones.

- Do not run a swab through a hard rubber mouthpiece. Gently clean it with a separate cloth.

■ *Temperature*

- To avoid cracking, *never blow warm air down a cold wood instrument to warm it up.* Warm it from the outside by leaving it in a warm room or holding it in hands or near the body.

- Wood instruments should not be exposed to extremes of heat or cold. Never leave a wood instrument in a car in the heat of summer or the cold of winter or in a room where extremes of temperature or humidity are experienced.

■ *Assembly and Handling*

- Do not grab a joint in such a way that keys that are not designed to be depressed directly by the fingers are being depressed or torqued in the twisting process.

- Begin assembling from the bell, foot joint or butt joint of the instrument working toward the mouthpiece, and disassemble in reverse order from assembly.

- Oboes, clarinets, bassoons and saxophones have "bridge keys," which transfer motion from one joint to another. These are delicate and are easily thrown out of adjustment—always raise the upper member of the "bridge" when assembling and be careful not to twist too far and bend the key. Protect any cork or other material the two halves of the bridge mechanism join.

- For larger clarinets (bass or contra), saxophones, and bassoons, work with the case in front or beside you on the floor, rather than in your lap.

- Woodwind instruments—especially larger ones—nested in the case can be thrown out of adjustment by simply jarring the case or setting it down with too much force. Carry and set cases down carefully.

- Do not over-tighten a ligature. A drop of oil on the threads of ligature screws protects the threads from stripping and prolongs the ligature's life.

- Lift the saxophone by the bell and not by the narrow upper end of the instrument over the keys.

- Using wood instruments on a marching field greatly increases the risk of cracking.

Troubleshooting

Testing Student Instruments

- Where possible, test the joints of a woodwind instrument by plugging the end and all holes and sucking the air out of the joint. A joint should hold a vacuum for a short period of time.

- To avoid viruses and bacteria that incubate in schools, own oboe and bassoon reeds, and clarinet and saxophone mouthpieces and reeds in which you have confidence to use when trying students' instruments. A good (Leger) polymer single reed is a viable option that will last for years under this kind of use. Your other option is to own one of the available disinfectant sprays that are used for instrument demonstrations when elementary school students are recruited for the middle school band program. These may be ordered from Ferree's Tools, Inc.

"Lost motion" (loose keys—a job for a repair technician)

- Over time, woodwind keys wear at the ends where they meet the posts and some up-and-down motion ("free" or "lost" motion) develops. This lost motion needs to be eliminated to quiet the keys and so that the pad will always rest on the seating ring in exactly the same location.

- If a solid key is hinged on pivot screws, some metal is removed from the post with a countersink so that the screws reach farther into the indentations at the ends of the keys.

- If the key and touchpiece are mounted on a hollow tube with a rod running the length of the key, the metal of the tube itself is stretched or "swedged" with a swedging plier.

Producing a tone becomes more difficult as more fingers are put down

- A pad or several pads are leaking. Test the joints to be sure they hold a vacuum by plugging or closing all of the holes and sucking the air out of the joint. The joint of a small instrument should hold a vacuum for several seconds at least, and the joint of a large instrument should produce a discernable vacuum. Larger instrument with leather or composition pads may be checked with a leak light.

The instrument can be played from the shortest fingering downward only to a certain point

- A pad is either missing or not sealing the tone hole at about the location of the lowest finger in the last successful fingering. Sometimes this happens when a bridge key as on clarinet or oboe is bent, an adjustment screw inadequately adjusted as on saxophone, or some other key is bent.

Rod-axels or pivot screws loose

- As long as tightening the pivot screw all the way does not cause the key to bind, it should be tightened all the way. Do not confuse a pivot or rod axel with an adjustment screw, as on flutes, oboes, the A key on clarinets and the G# key on saxophones.

- If a screw continues to work its way loose, put some beeswax on the threads of the screw.

Adjustment screws misaligned

- When closing one pad ("master") causes a pad above it ("slave") to also close, both must rest on the seating ring with equal pressure. Test with a small strip of cigarette paper (oboe, clarinet, flute, bassoon) or a leak light (saxophone, bassoon, bass clarinet). Always start from the top of the instrument and work your way down.

Needle springs unhooked

- Use a spring hook or small crochet hook to restore the needle spring to its saddle.

Needle springs broken

- A rubber band can provide a temporary solution, but specialized tools and a technician are required to replace the spring.

Flat springs loose or fallen off

- Tighten or replace the screw that holds the flat spring on the key. When you remove the tiny screws that are either pivots or attachment screws for flat springs, use a "refrigerator magnet" such as one used to attach advertisement to a metal surface as a working surface to avoid losing screws.

Pad has fallen out

- To re-cement the same pad in an emergency, the exact position of the seating ring must be rediscovered before melting the shellac or cement to reattach the pad. Hold the instrument so that gravity holds the pad in the key cup and test the pad with cigarette paper or a leak light in many positions of rotation until a seat around the whole circumference is discovered. Then, close the key and heat the pad from the side with a clean flame such as alcohol lamp, butane lighter or bunsen burner.

- The best option is to replace the pad with a new one. If using a bladder pad, carefully pierce the very edge of the pad with a needle to let out air as it heats. Melt enough cement to form a complete bed behind the pad and either apply it to the back of the pad or melt it in the removed key. With the key on the instrument, heat the pad in a closed position as shown on the following page until the pad moves into position parallel to the seating ring. When it cools, test all the way around the pad with a long, pointed piece of cigarette paper to be sure the pad seats in all places. You may need to reposition the pad slightly, heating and cooling again, until the pad seats.

- On a saxophone, the keys may have lacquer on them which will melt, and the buttons on the keys can burn or melt with heat, so unless you have fairly developed repair skills, leave this to a qualified repair technician.

Heating a bassoon pad from the side with a butane lighter

Heating a pad from the side to avoid burning the pad or the instrument

Pad seats poorly and leaks

- A pad will leak when the cigarette paper pulls tightly in one part of the circumference of the seating ring and not in others. It may be simpler to replace the pad with a new one that has no seating ring pressed into it.

Pad has split or the skin has come off

- Replace the pad.

Sticky pads

- Pads occasionally stick to the instrument, either causing the pad to lift too slowly (articulated G# on saxophone or bass clarinet) or to not come up at all. Insert a clean piece of paper (e.g. non-gummed cigarette paper) between the pad and the instrument, hold the pad down to the instrument, and pull the paper out. It may be necessary to use a small amount of rubbing alcohol to clean the seating ring on the instrument. If the pad continues to stick, a small amount of baby powder on the pad may solve the problem.

Checking a pad for even seal
around circumference
of the seating ring

A tenon cork or saxophone neck cork has fallen off or is too loose

- Re-gluing the old cork is hardly ever satisfactory. For a temporary repair, wrap the tenon or saxophone neck with waxed dental floss to serve until the instrument arrives at the repair shop.

- Replace with a new cork by measuring sheet cork to the correct width, beveling one end, applying contact cement to the back and bevel of the cork and to the area to which you intend to attach the cork and letting the contact cement dry. In about fifteen minutes, wrap the cork around the tenon or neck, lapping the glued side over the glued bevel. Sand down to size with sandpaper.

- Sometimes wrapping a small strip of paper around the cork and putting the mouthpiece over it as a shim makes a satisfactory temporary repair.

Cork bumper has fallen off

- Striker corks and felts are held on with contact cement—follow the instructions on the bottle or tube. Re-gluing a dry, old cork is rarely satisfactory. Cement a larger piece of cork onto the key and then trim to size with a single-edge razor blade.

A wood instrument (oboe, clarinet, piccolo) has cracked

- Stop playing the instrument and mark the crack with a pencil—draw a line over the crack and perpendicular lines at the ends of the crack showing its exact location and total length so that the crack can be identified if it closes before the technician sees it. *The crack should be pinned and not flush-banded.* Pins are screws embedded in the wood across the crack at diagonals to stabilize the instrument and prevent further movement. Pinning allows the instrument to swell and contract around that point, whereas flush banding does not, causing the relationships of bore dimension to change with the weather and season.

- If the crack goes into a tone hole, have the hole drilled out and a plastic tone hole bushing inserted and a new pad installed so that the instrument will never leak if the crack opens again.

Basic Woodwind Toolbox

Many of the following items are available in various local markets. Specialized tools are easily found under *Woodwind Instrument Repair Tools* on the Internet.

Waterproof (Wetordry) sandpaper, 240 and 400 grit
Small swivel-top screwdrivers (flat)
Pair small toothless pliers
Small crochet hook or spring hook
Piece of one-quarter inch thick glass with edges smoothed or plexiglass
Cork grease
Waxed dental floss
Small bottle or tube of contact cement (available in hardware stores)
Stick of French cement or stick shellac (for pad replacement)
Package of non-gummed cigarette paper
Single-edged razor blades
Source of heat such as an alcohol lamp with denatured alcohol or a butane lighter, (which unlike matches, will not leave a carbon deposit on the key).
Scissors

Woodwind key oil or an oiler with clean motor oil

Bore oil and a chamois swab dedicated to oil (Once it is used to oil an instrument, it can no longer be used for cleaning).

Clear finger nail polish (to stabilize unraveling string on oboe or bassoon reeds)

Pad slick (pad leveling tool)

Needle or safety pin

Tweezers

Cork Grease

Flute cleaning rod

A supply of pads, corks, and springs, as included in a ready-made repair kit (below)

Large flat magnet such as one designed to hold advertising on a refrigerator door

Mouthpieces and reeds for all common woodwinds

More advanced:

Reed knife

Oboe plaque

Bassoon plaque or guitar pick

Repair kits which include the bulk of the above already supplied are available from Ferree's Tools, Inc (*www.ferreestools.com*).

Tuning

For a detailed discussion of wind instrument intonation, see Shelly Jagow's book, *Tuning for Wind Instruments: A Roadmap to Successful Intonation* (Meredith Music Publications).

■ When tuning in an ensemble, always check more than one note on a woodwind instrument, and *always tune in the middle of the dynamic range*. Dynamic affects pitch on different instruments differently.

■ Wind instruments play sharper when they are warm and flatter when they are cold. Woodwind instruments are built to play at or very near a specific level of pitch—usually A=440 in the U.S. or slightly higher in Europe.

■ On all wind instruments, shortening the tube makes the instrument sharper and lengthening it makes it flatter. Lengthening the tube near the source of vibration flattens the short fingerings (notes which have the fewest fingers down) more than it flattens the longer fingerings (those with more fingers down).

■ Do not pull out the mouthpiece on clarinet or the reed on oboe.

■ Be aware of how high pads lift off of instruments and how dirt in tone holes affects individual notes. A considerable amount of accumulated dirt inside a tone hole will make the note emitting from that hole (i.e. when that hole is the highest open hole on the instrument) flat. Pad height is also critical—most often one experiences a flat note which may also "wheeze" or sound dull as a result of the pad not opening sufficiently.

FLUTE AND PICCOLO

Purchasing

■ *Options*

■ Most beginning flutes have closed tone holes (*plateau,* as opposed to open or French model), and C foot joints (as opposed to B). Some makers supply a curved head joint, a "wave" head joint, or a straight one, so that a very small student can manage the instrument.

Headjoint accommodations for small players
(Reprinted courtesy of Jupiter Band Instruments)

■ Open-hole flutes are available as beginners' instruments. The argument is that open holes automatically force good hand position. These flutes will be supplied with plugs for the tone holes, making the instrument as easy to play as the plateau model with imperfect hand position. The last plug can be left in the G key only, so that L3 closes more easily, though all plugs should be eliminated as soon as possible.

- In-line or offset G key is also available—the advantage of the offset G is that L3 does not have to reach as far to close the key. Offset G is widely preferred because of ergonomics and resale value.

In-line G key   Offset G key

(Reprinted courtesy of Miyazawa)

■ *Recommended student flute brands*

- Yamaha, (both closed and open-hole)

- Gemeinhardt, Models 3, 2SP and 2SH

- Jupiter, (515S with curved head joint, 511 with B foot joint, and 515RS)

- Armstrong

■ *Step-up*

- The second flute and every flute that a student owns thereafter should be an open-hole, or French model with a low B foot joint. In addition to assuring good hand position, the advantages are that more sound is allowed to emit from the instrument, the scale is more even, and one has more control of the air column for advanced or extended techniques. In addition to adding one low note to the range, the B foot joint provides additional resonance and stability to certain notes, high C in particular. An extension to the low B key called a "gizmo" is found on most B foot joints.

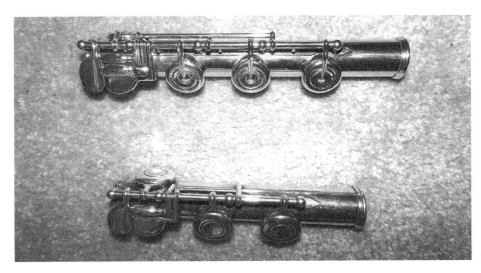

B foot joint (above) with gizmo and C foot joint (below)

Recommended step-up brands

- Virtually all of the top makers of professional models also have a "student" model, referring to the first step-up flute after the one that the middle school student played for under $1000.00.

- Yamaha flutes and piccolos are safe at any price point, from the beginning models all the way through the 14K gold model flute which is comparable in price to the most expensive American professional model flutes.

Professional models

- At the highest levels, the Boston makers Haynes and Powell are the older established names, with other American makers Altes, Lillian Burkart and Brannen flutes enjoying wide popularity. The Japanese makers Muramatsu, Miyazawa, Nagahara and Sankyo have also risen to this level.

- Piccolos made by these makers and Hammig are highly recommended.

Maintenance and Storage

■ *Moisture Removal*

- Swab the inside to remove moisture before returning the instrument to the case. Do not store the wet swabbing cloth inside the bore of the instrument. Insert the corner of a soft, lint-free handkerchief into the eye of the cleaning rod. Drape the handkerchief over the end of the rod to prevent it from scratching the inside of the flute. Swab each joint individually.

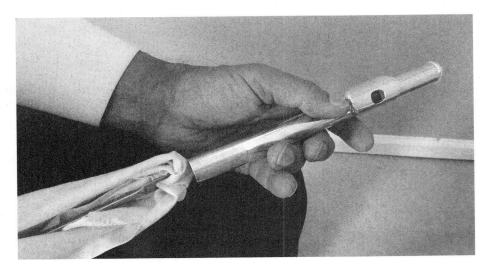

Swabbing to avoid scratching the bore

■ *Lubricants and Polishes*

- ■ Please see "Woodwinds in General."

- ■ Clean the tenon with rubbing alcohol for small dirt accumulation or with very fine steel wool for greater accumulations.

- ■ Do not use cork grease on flute tenons or on the headjoint cork.

■ *Storage*

- ■ Store the instrument in the case designed for the instrument.

- ■ Avoid extreme heat (as in a closed car in the summer, direct sunlight, etc.) which might render the glue on trill or C pads malleable.

Troubleshooting

For the following topics, please see "Woodwinds in General"

- ■ Lost Motion (loose keys)
- ■ Needle Springs Unhooked
- ■ Needle Springs Broken
- ■ Flat Springs Loose or Fallen Off
- ■ Pad has fallen out
- ■ Pad seats poorly and leaks
- ■ Pad has split or the skin has come off
- ■ Sticky pads
- ■ Cork bumper has fallen off
- ■ Basic Woodwind Toolbox
- ■ Pads missing
- ■ Pads leaking
- ■ Pads sticking
- ■ Testing student instruments
- ■ Rod axels or pivot screws loose

■ *Pitch*

Flatness Overall

- Head joint may be pulled out too far. The headjoint should be pulled out slightly, but this can be overdone.

- Head joint cork may be too far up the flute (toward the crown). Check it with the line on the end of the cleaning rod as shown below:

- Student may be rolling in too far, often the result of poor posture. Cover ⅓ of the blowhole in the low register only. See WOODWIND METHODS . . .

Flatness at soft dynamics

- The air speed is too slow, the aperture is too large to accelerate the air stream, or the air stream is directed too much in the downward direction.

Sharpness overall

- Not enough of the blowhole is being covered. Generally about ⅓ of the hole should be covered in the lower register, and more than that covered in higher registers.

line

- Check also the head joint cork, to be sure that the line on the cleaning rod is not too far down the flute (away from the crown).

Headjoint with cleaning rod line in the middle of the blowhole

- (Professional model flutes are built at various pitch levels—generally A=440, 442 or 444). When shopping for a flute, be sure you are aware of the pitch level at which the instrument is built.

Individual notes only are out of tune with the rest of the scale

- Student may be using an incorrect fingering, since wrong fingerings *almost* work on the flute. See WOODWIND METHODS, Flute, Common Problems.

- A pad may not be rising far enough off the instrument to sufficiently vent the note. This will happen if a key has been bent, if the striker has been bent or the striker cork is missing or has been replaced by a pad or cork of improper thickness.

■ *Response*

Instrument generally responds poorly

- Check first for pads which are torn, with skin missing, or are moth-eaten and replace if needed.

- If long fingerings respond worse than short fingerings, check for leakage in pads by using feeler gauges made of strips of ungummed cigarette paper. Place the feeler between the pad and the tone hole and gently hold the key down while pulling the paper out. You should feel even resistance around the circumferences of all pads. An individual pad not seating requires a technician.

- The easiest kind of leaks to resolve on a flute are when two or more keys are moved by the same finger stroke. Be sure all pads seat individually first. Find the small set screw where the motion is transferred from one key to the other and make the adjustment. (Often, professional model flutes do not have adjustment screws, and so these adjustments are made by a technician by adjusting cork thicknesses at the points where the motion transfers from the "master" pad to the "slave" pad. In this case it is a problem for a technician.)

Checking for leaks in pads and for identical seating of master and slave pads

- Be sure the head joint cork is in the right place. When a head joint cork gets very old it becomes loose and will slide up the headjoint toward the crown, and if it has shrunk badly, it will leak.

- There may be space between the headjoint cork and the metal face plate just above the blowhole. Be sure the threaded nut on the upper (toward the crown) end of the cork is snug against the cork itself and pulls the face plate tight against the cork. If the cork has shrunk it will require a new headjoint cork.

High notes do not speak (especially piccolo)

- Particularly on piccolo this is a problem with pressure into the lip or embouchure tension. See WOODWIND METHODS

■ Mechanical

Tenons too loose or too tight

- Male tenon has dirt or corrosion. Clean with very fine steel wool.

- If the resistance is only slight and the tenon is clean, apply a little candle wax to the male tenon. If too loose, a thickness of scotch tape can stabilize the tenon temporarily.

- Male tenon has been damaged. A technician uses specialized tools to expand or contract the male end as well as restore the roundness.

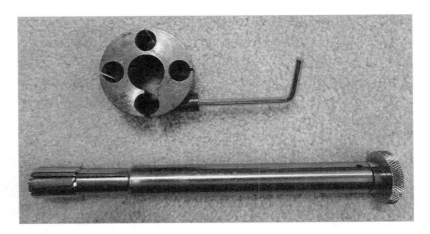

Flute tenon contraction and expansion tools

Bent keys, causing pads to seat on one side but not the other or to bind

- Unless you have considerable repair skills, send the flute to a quality repair shop.

Instrument has become tarnished

- Use a polishing cloth designed for this purpose. Never use silver polish on a wind instrument.

Dents in the body or headjoint

- A job for a repair technician. Done with a burnishing rod and a headjoint or body mandrel

Instrument constantly goes out of adjustment

- If the tenons are too tight, the player may be putting excessive pressure on the keys and pads.

- Be sure the instrument is nested securely in the case—preferably one made for that instrument.

OBOE AND ENGLISH HORN

Purchasing

■ *Options*

■ The least expensive plastic oboes will lack low B-flat keys, left-hand F key, and F resonance key and may feel somewhat unstable—especially on Forked F. Unless a compelling financial reason exists to shop the "bargain basement" for school inventory, consider the importance of your oboist to your long-term instrumentation and get the best possible plastic instrument.

Left-hand F and low B-flat key

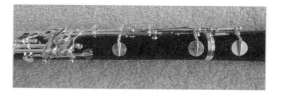

F resonance key
(below R4 touchpieces)

■ English horns have the same options as oboes with the exception of low B-flat.

■ *Recommended beginning and intermediate brands*

■ The Fox Company dominates this market, with their Renard student models. Plastic is strongly recommended for young oboists to avoid problems with cracking.

Yamaha

Howarth

Buffet Prodige

Cabart (the student model of the Loree company).

■ *Professional oboes*

- ■ Grenadilla wood is most common, though with high incidence of cracking. Greenline (Buffet's combination of grenadilla sawdust and bonding agents) is more durable and is gaining significant acceptance in the profession. Loree, Howarth and others make a plastic upper joint and grenadilla lower joint and bell, which resolves most cracking concerns.

- ■ Recommended brands:

    Loree dominates this market with the basic Loree Paris professional oboe and the Loree Paris Royal oboe

    Laubin

    Fox

    Buffet (Orfeo)

    Howarth

    Marigaux

Maintenance and Storage

■ *Moisture*

- ■ Swab regularly with a swab with a weighted cord, a cloth and a length of cord trailing the cloth to avoid stuck swabs, or use a turkey tail feather.

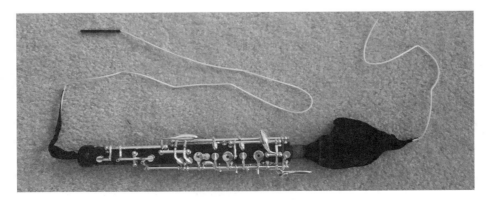

Upper joint with swab

- Moisture is most problematic in the upper joint. The octave key holes are so small that a seamstress's pin will not fit into them, so the tiniest amount of water will cause the upper octave fingerings to either speak in the lower octave or to break intermittently into the lower octave. To remove water from octave keys, place cigarette paper between the octave key pad and the hole, plug the end and close the holes and blow while opening and closing the octave key.

- When wood absorbs moisture in the interior bore causing the interior to swell more than the exterior, a wood joint may crack. With a new oboe especially, swab often to minimize the introduction of moisture into the wood, thereby minimizing the likelihood of the instrument cracking.

- See also Oiling the wood, under Lubricants and Polishes in "Woodwinds in General"

Clearing octave keys of water

Oiling keys

- All woodwind keys require lubrication. See "Oiling Keys" in "Woodwinds in General."

Temperature and humidity

- Store wood oboes in a room free from extremes of temperature or humidity.

- Upper joints of oboes are where most cracks develop, commonly caused by blowing warm, moist air down a cold, dry instrument. The advice found on some band folders: "Warm your instrument by blowing warm air through it before you play" is *very bad* advice for someone with a wooden instrument. Always warm a wood instrument with your body heat from the outside of the instrument.

Troubleshooting

For the following topics, please see "Woodwinds in General"

- Lubricants and Polishes
- Lost Motion (loose keys)
- Needle Springs Unhooked
- Needle Springs Broken
- Flat Springs Loose or Fallen Off
- Pad has fallen out
- Pad seats poorly and leaks
- Pad has split or the skin has come off
- Sticky pads
- Cork bumper has fallen off
- Basic Woodwind Toolbox
- Pads missing
- Pads leaking
- Pads sticking
- Tenon cork or neck cork too loose or missing
- Testing student instruments
- Rod axels or pivot screws loose

■ *Pitch*

- The way the oboe reed is scraped affects the pitch. A shorter scraped area may play sharp. In this case, scraping between the center and the sides in the back third to lengthen the "W" design will allow the reed to play lower and will also make the lower register respond more easily.
- If scraping, avoid thinning the spine of the reed, or the upper register will play flat and the reed must be discarded.

Pitch is sharp overall

- The student may have too much reed in the mouth or may be pinching the reed. See WOODWIND METHODS pp. 28-32 and 20b "Oboe tone development" exercises. *(Since the most common error young students make is taking too much reed into the mouth, pulling the reed out of the well only allows the student to continue with a bad habit, it creates problems within the scale itself, and the tone will never develop. When you ask an oboist to "pull out," be clear that you mean "pull it out of your mouth," and not out of the oboe.)*

- If the reed is shorter than 70mm, then the reed is too short.

- There may be too much bark on the back ⅓ of the reed. Lengthen the scrape by scraping between the center and the sides in the back third of the reed, deepening the "W" shape in the scrape.

Pitch is flat overall

- The reed may not be inserted all the way into the reed well, probably because the cork is new and too thick. Compress the cork as shown below and push it in until you feel it hit the bottom of the well.

- The student may not be blowing strongly enough.

- The reed could be too long. The standard oboe reed is 70mm long, and the standard staple (the metal tube upon which the blades of the reed are tied) length 47mm, though staples may be bought that are shorter. If flatness is a consistent problem with 47mm staples, seek reeds tied on 45mm staples.

- The reed may be too soft, i.e. too much wood has been scraped from the reed.

Pitch is flat in the upper register

- The reed is either much too soft or the spine of the reed has been scraped through.

Pitch of certain notes is inconsistent with the rest of the scale

- Wrong fingerings almost produce the right notes on the oboe, though often the sound and pitch do not match the rest of the notes in the scale. There are many common mistakes that oboe students make—see "Common Problems" and "Oboe Fingering Chart Commentary" in WOODWIND METHODS.

- Dirt or lint may have accumulated in a tone hole.

- There may not be sufficient clearance between a pad and the tone hole, making the note emitting from that hole flat. If a technician has used a pad which is too thick or a striker cork that is too thick, the pad will rest too near the instrument and the note emitting will be flat. A striker cork can be sanded: a pad which is too thick should be replaced.

- E-natural is unstable. Check to see if the plaque slides in between the blades unusually easily and if so, *some* oboists (a minority) advocate closing the reed by crimping the tube gently with pliers. With the mandrel in the reed almost all the way, apply toothless pliers to the tube at a perpendicular to the tip opening about 2 mm. below the highest wrap of string and squeeze gently. This should push the blades together and stabilize the E. If this happens with all reeds, the problem is the bell and not the reed.

- E-natural (4th space) is unstable with all reeds. Insert a length of electrician's tape high inside the bell longitudinally to add stability or find a bell that solves this problem.

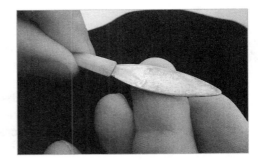

Inserting plaque without risking damage to tip

- E-natural (4th space) is sensitive to different bell shapes and to anything (such as the player's knee) close to the bell opening. Be sure the bell is clear of all obstructions, even partial ones.

- E-natural (4th space) might be flat if someone has altered the interior of the bell (perhaps with too much tape) or to stabilize that note or if an inappropriate bell is being used. Remove some of the tape or try another bell.

High C# and D are sharp to the rest of the scale

- The low C key holds the middle touchpiece on the lower joint (2R) down. If that touchpiece does not go down completely, these notes can be sharp. Adjust the screw on the C key and test the two pads with cigarette paper to be sure they are seating with identical resistance and pressure. (However, some oboists prefer to leave this coupling slightly out of adjustment for pitch or response reasons.)

Only high C# is flat or sharp to the rest of the scale

- The half-hole touchpiece (1L) rests too far (sharp) or too near (flat) the hole. If there is a screw on the striker side of that key, turn to adjust the height of the pad until it can be played in tune. On a very inexpensive oboe, the thickness off the striker cork on 1L should be adjusted.

■ *Response*

Notes at the bottom of and below the staff do not speak

- The oboe is out of adjustment. Be sure both joints hold a vacuum when all the holes and end are plugged and the air is drawn out. If one or the other joint does not hold a vacuum, see a technician.

Vacuum testing upper joint

- Testing for adjustment is more complicated on oboe than the other woodwinds because depressing the top pad on the lower joint raises rather than lowers pads on the upper. These are put down again by combinations operated by the left hand fingers. Starting from the top of the oboe or English horn, hold the 1R pad down and then depress the 2L touchpiece to ascertain that 2L and the pad above it touch equally when tested with a cigarette paper strip. (see Woodwinds in General). Turn the adjustment screw where the motion is transferred between these two keys until the two pads rest on the tone holes equally. Work your way down from the top of the instrument, checking all combinations for equal pressure. (While oboe adjustment may seem complicated at first, the guidance of an experienced technician or oboist reveals very simple logic of this procedure).

- Poor reed. Lower register notes will not work if there are no "lows" in the crow when the reed is inserted into the mouth beyond the strings. Lengthen the "W" scrape by removing wood closer to the strings.

- Wire on the reed. While wires on English horn reeds and bassoon reeds are necessary, they can be a hindrance on an oboe reed. Carefully removing the wire often improves the reed by allowing the back to vibrate.

- Poorly cut reed. A reed needs to have a well-defined tip, a heart and a spine. If the design of the reed does not include these three features, a different design of reed should be sought.

- Insufficient soaking can cause the tip to be too closed and thus the reed will only have high pitches

- Dirt may have accumulated inside the reed. Use a clean pipe cleaner, insert it in the bottom end of the reed and pull it through without reversing directions.

- Other "fixes" for a reed that does not crow require the experience and tools of a specialist. Change reeds.

Notes above the staff do not speak

- The reed may be too soft or the tip may be too long. A very small amount of the tip may be removed with a single-edged razor blade.

Only certain notes do not speak

- Check adjustment as described above.

Tone is too bright

- Player may have too much reed in the mouth.

- A reed which has too little heart will be too bright.

Tone is fuzzy

- Most likely there is too much wood still in the reed. Try a reed which is one step softer.

Short fingerings play but long fingerings do not

◼ There is a leaking pad somewhere below the highest open hole on the last good note. Be sure the two joints hold a vacuum, and see "The oboe is out of adjustment" above.

The reed crows, but many or most notes don't speak

◼ Be sure the reed is not leaking air near the strings. Plug the end and force air into the tip with your mouth to test for leakage between the blades. Sometimes, putting Goldbeater's skin or plastic wrap at the base of the cane and wrapping over some of the strings will seal the leak

◼ Be sure reed has sufficient tip and the tip is the same length on both blades of the reed.

◼ Lengthen the tip (the final 4mm. where the light shines through most brightly) if necessary. Or find reeds with longer tips. A longer tip will respond more easily.

◼ *Mechanical*

Reed (staple) does not fit into the oboe

◼ If the staple fits too tightly into the oboe, or if it does not go down all the way into the reed well, roll the tube between a flat surface and a reed knife or table knife to compress the cork slightly. Do not use cork grease on the reed, as the inadvertent transfer of cork grease to the blades of the reed will waterproof the outside of the reed, making the reed much more closed.

◼ If the staple does not fit tightly enough, soak the cork in water until it expands sufficiently to fit securely into the well. Heating the cork will also cause it to expand, but only temporarily.

Rolling the tube to compress staple cork

Stuck swab

◼ The swab should be pulled back through the large end of the joint. Ideally, use a swab that has a piece of cord that trails beyond the end of the swab so that if stuck, it can be easily pulled backwards out of the larger end of the bore (see picture under "Maintenance and Storage).

- Better yet, insert the swab from the narrow top end and pull it out the large end, which completely eliminates the possibility of the swab getting stuck.

- Never try to work the swab out by inserting a tool in any tone hole.

Cracks (usually in the upper joint)
- See "Woodwinds in General."

English Horn

■ *Purchasing*

- For school use, silver keys and grenadilla wood are unnecessary. Plastic is highly recommended, especially for the upper joint to avoid risk of cracking. Fox (Renard) dominates the school market, with the Renard 555.

- Fox instruments, in maple, grenadilla wood, plastic, and a combination also recommended. Fox 520 is plastic and Fox 510 is grenadilla lower and bell with plastic upper joint, which largely solves the cracking problem. The other two Fox models are maple and grenadilla, which are excellent but the risk of cracking is significant.

- Loree's student-level Cabart instrument (wood) is also excellent but wood carries the risk of cracking.

- The professional market is virtually dominated by Loree, with three professional models. Most oboe manufacturers also make an English horn—Howarth, Marigaux, Buffet, Laubin, etc. Some have waiting lists several years long.

■ *Other issues*

- No. 2 bocal is the standard length. A lower number is a shorter bocal and a higher number is longer.

- Fourth-space "C" (concert F) may drop in pitch as the player plays softly. This is a bocal issue—try another bocal. The "Dallas" bocal was designed to correct this problem, but professional advice is recommended to match any bocal to an instrument.

- In the very highest (altissimo) register of English horn, players often develop a set of fingerings that respond and tune better than standard oboe fingerings.

- A neck strap may be used to offset the weight of the English horn.

Oboe and English Horn Reeds

■ *Recommended Suppliers for Oboe Reeds*

■ Forrests, the Double Reed Specialists
1849 University Ave.
Berkeley, CA 94703 U.S.A.
(510) 845-7178
sales@forrestsmusic.com

■ RDG Woodwinds, Inc.
589 North Larchmont Blvd., 2nd Floor
Los Angeles, CA 90004
(323)463-4930

General reed knowledge for the non-oboist

■ All cane (organic) reeds react to changes of altitude, barometric pressure, humidity, and weather. A reed made in Florida and sold as "medium" feels harder when played in Colorado, and most reeds play more poorly on stormy days.

■ Generally oboe reeds are made on a 47mm staple and are 70mm in overall length. One can make a shorter reed to play sharper, but it should be on a shorter staple, for example 45mm, otherwise the tone and response will suffer.

■ The threads that hold the cane on the staple should go exactly to the end of the staple, so one can be fairly certain that the exterior measurement from the bottom end to the top thread is the length of the staple.

■ An oboe reed needs to have a discernable tip—a thinner area in the last 4–5mm of the reed. Avoid commercial reeds that have a gradual slope, more like a clarinet or saxophone reed.

■ The features of a well-designed oboe reed are discernible tip about 4mm. long, a heart—a somewhat thicker area behind the tip—a spine, and a "W" shaped scrape in the back ⅓ of the reed. These features can be seen by holding the reed between a light source and your eye.

■ The wood part and a small portion of the strings of the reed should be soaked in water (as opposed to saliva). Since wood expands toward moisture, mouth soaking will cause the reed to be excessively open and may deteriorate the reed cane more quickly.

Oboe reed, showing spine, "W," tip and heart

- A new reed will absorb water quickly; an older one will take longer to soak.

- Warmer water will soak a reed more quickly than cold. Generally avoid ice-cold water.

- "Crowing" is when the reed is inserted all the way into the mouth to the strings, with no contact between wood and lip. *This is not an oboe embouchure*—it is merely a way to know that the reed will produce both high and low sounds when allowed to vibrate in an uncontrolled fashion. It may be necessary to open a reed by gently squeezing it sideways near the strings, or it may be necessary to close it by squeezing it closed at the tip before it will crow.

Soaking an oboe reed just past the strings

- Some reeds are designed so that one side plays better than the other. Test the reed with both blades uppermost and remember which way it plays best.

- Sometimes reeds develop a split in one of the blades. If the split is toward the center of the blade, the reed probably is ruined. Sometimes a reed which is split closer to the side of the blade will continue to function.

- Before removing wood with a reed knife, an oboe plaque should be gently placed between the blades of an oboe reed. Do not push the plaque in very far, or you run the risk of tearing a hole in the side of the reed, between the blades. A reed knife is used for scraping rather than cutting or carving, and thus the blade is held more or less perpendicular rather than at an oblique angle to the reed.

CLARINET

Purchasing

All student and entry-level professional model clarinets have the same basic options—seventeen keys, six rings, Boehm fingering system. Plastic is much more stable and durable than wood for student clarinets, so virtually all modern student clarinets are plastic.

■ *Recommended student clarinet brands*

- Buffet, B-12, BC2539-2-0
- Yamaha, YCL255
- Conn-Selmer, including Vito 7212PC and Selmer
- Jupiter JCL-700

■ *Step-up between beginning and professional instruments*

- Retain the plastic beginner instrument for marching band to preserve the more expensive instrument.
- Traditionally, grenadilla wood , but Greenline, Buffet's mixture of powdered grenadilla and resin, is now endorsed by many leading clarinetists, bass clarinetists and oboists. The likelihood of developing a crack is virtually non-existent.
- Among the best step-up instruments are Buffet , Yamaha and Selmer.
- Buffet E-11, E-12, E-13, Yamaha YCL-450, Selmer CL-211.

Professional instruments
- Please read "Instrument Selection" in "Woodwinds in General." Regardless of the model and make preferred, look for (1) an

appealing sound, (2) evenness of sound throughout the scale with no notes "jumping out" or sounding more muffled than others, and (3) very good intonation. *Always* take a tuner to try woodwind instruments.

- Buffet R-13, Selmer Signature or Yamaha YCL-CSVR are entry-level professional instruments. Because Buffet dominates the professional market in the U.S. with the R-13, the resale values are attractive.

- Some of these instruments, for example, the Selmer Recital series, weigh more than others, so in some cases an elastic neck strap is a worthwhile investment.

- Other (more elaborate) options at higher price points include left-hand A-flat/E-flat key, more choice heartwood, a choice of nickel or silver plated keys, variations in the undercutting of tone holes, and fancier case. Buffet Prestige R-13, RC, Festival, Tosca, Divine and Tradition, Selmer Signature.

- Different mouthpieces and barrels alter intonation relationships, both within the instrument's own scale and overall.

Maintenance and Storage

- Swab after every use and also intermittently while playing to keep condensation from leaking out of holes—especially those on the back side of the instrument. Remove the mouthpiece. Invert the instrument, and be sure the cloth or chamois swab is not folded to ensure that it will not become stuck on the register key tube. Swab the mouthpiece separately.

- To prevent cracks, new wood clarinets should be swabbed very frequently to ensure that the interior of the clarinet does not absorb water and expand more quickly than the exterior.

- Apply cork grease to tenon corks to lubricate and also to the wood at the very end and even down inside the bore of new upper male tenons to keep water from soaking into the open-end grains of the wood.

- Lubrication—see "Lubricants and Polishes" and "Oiling Wood Instruments" in "Woodwinds in General."

- Periodically check how the pads seal by closing the lower end of each joint, closing all of the holes, and sucking the air out of the joint. If the joint does not hold a vacuum for several seconds, one or more pads is leaking. If the pad can be identified with a cigarette paper feeler, replace the pad. Or take the instrument to a technician.

Testing pads by
drawing a vacuum
(above)
and
by feeling with cigarette paper
(right).

■ Periodically, tone holes need to be cleaned with a cotton swab. Keys may be removed to gain access to holes that collect dirt—especially those high on the upper joint. A very tiny amount of rubbing alcohol may be used but, there is a dye on the wood of less expensive clarinets that alcohol will dissolve.

■ *Wood instruments that are cold should be warmed from the outside—not by blowing warm air into them.* Do not expose wood instruments to extremes of heat or cold.

Troubleshooting

For the following topics, please see "Woodwinds in General"

■ Lubricants and Polishes

■ Lost Motion (loose keys)

- Needle Springs Unhooked
- Needle Springs Broken
- Flat Springs Loose or Fallen Off
- Pad has fallen out
- Pad seats poorly and leaks
- Pad has split or the skin has come off
- Sticky pads
- Cork bumper has fallen off
- Basic Woodwind Toolbox
- Pads missing
- Pads leaking
- Pads sticking
- Tenon cork or neck cork too loose or missing
- Testing student instruments
- Rod axels or pivot screws loose.
- Basic woodwind tool box

■ *Pitch*

General comments

- Clarinet pitch is the least flexible of the woodwinds, with some potential to push ("lip") the pitch downward, but with very little flexibility upward.
- The natural tendency is to be sharper at soft dynamics and flatter at loud ones in direct contrast to the flute.
- Also unlike the flute, the clarinet is sharp at the beginning of a breath and then the pitch "settles" because the initial air is less laden with carbon dioxide than it becomes after a second or two.

One register or group of pitches is flat or sharp to the rest of the clarinet's scale

- A barrel with a very narrow bore will cause the clarion register to be flatter to the lower register and one with a wider bore will do the opposite.
- A mouthpiece with a very large chamber can cause short fingerings—throat tones especially—to be very flat to the rest of the scale. *Always take a tuner with you when you try mouthpieces for purchase.*

Individual notes are out of tune with the rest of the scale

- Clarinetists have at their disposal numerous options for many notes, in the altissimo especially. Selecting the best fingering for a particular note in a passage may remove or reduce the need to manipulate the note with the embouchure.

- In the lower registers, a pitch problem that cannot be adjusted with the embouchure might be better addressed by altering a fingering— even putting an extra finger or key down some distance below the highest open hole, or by shading or slightly closing one of the open holes.

- For an exhaustive list of clarinet fingerings, see Thomas Ridenour's book, *Clarinet fingerings: A Guide for the Performer and Educator.*

Pitch is generally flat

- Different mouthpieces tune differently. If you are thoroughly committed to a particular mouthpiece and it is flat overall, the solution is to get a shorter barrel. Otherwise, look for a sharper mouthpiece.

- Shortening the mouthpiece tenon slightly is also a possibility, but is dangerous and requires specialized equipment.

Pitch is generally sharp

- See the comment above. A longer barrel or a different mouthpiece can adjust this.

- If the barrel needs to be pulled out a long way, inserting a tuning ring between the barrel and upper joint or the barrel and the mouthpiece (depending on the design of the tuning ring) will allow the increase in bore length without exaggerating the flatness of the throat tones. Tuning rings are the least expensive way to deal with a sharpness problem.

Tuning Rings

Pitch of short fingerings (many open holes) is flat or sharp to long fingerings (many holes closed)

- May have pulled out too far at the barrel and not enough between the hands.

- Often a mouthpiece issue. It is very common for a player to fall in love with a mouthpiece because of its sound and later realize that it cannot be played in tune.

- For best results, tune open G first by pulling at the barrel if G is sharp, and then bring the fourth space C the remaining distance downward by pulling between the upper and lower joints.

Pitch of one note is unusually flat and may "wheeze"

- Be sure the pad clears the highest open hole sufficiently.

- A cork pad will wheeze less than a pad covered with skin, especially if the edges of the cork pad have been trimmed or rounded.

- Check the highest open hole for accumulated dirt.

- See the resonance fingering discussions in WOODWIND METHODS for suggestions to minimize this issue.

Pitch of one note is unusually sharp, and brighter than the notes around it

- A key may be lifting the pad too high—probably because a striker cork has fallen off. This happens often on the throat A.

■ *Response and Annoying Noises*

Squeaks—The squeak is "duck-like"

- An unintended harmonic. Assuming all pads seal, the problem probably is tongue position or embouchure. See "Common Problems" in WOODWIND METHODS.

- If the upper joint does not hold a vacuum, these squeaks will be more unavoidable.

Squeaks—the squeak is high and whistle-like at the very beginning of the attack" (Pressure squeak)

- Possibly a thin spot or a split in the tip of the reed.

- If all reeds "whistle" in this way, the mouthpiece facing is worn or damaged. Light reflected off the rails should not show an obvious inward tilt or rounding at the fulcrum point, about a half inch from the tip. If "rail tilt" is present, replace or reface the mouthpiece.

- Mouthpieces with very thin side rails are inclined to whistle in this way also. (This is especially true of certain jazz tenor saxophone mouthpieces).

The tone lacks focus—"spreads" and perhaps sounds a bit saxophone-like

- The tongue position incorrect. See WOODWIND METHODS: Common Problems.

- There is leakage high in the upper joint, especially on the higher trill keys or G# and A keys.

- The ligature is too low or is too loose to hold the stock of the reed firmly.

- The reed is too wide and needs to be gently sanded on the sides to narrow it. However, be absolutely sure the sides remain perfectly straight.

- The reed is much too soft.

- If the barrel joint is wood, it may be worn out. Try some new barrels. If many or all of them resolve the issue, replace the barrel joint.

Low C# (and perhaps G# a twelfth above) wheezes

- The C#/G# hole is drilled too high and too small to be acoustically correct to avoid the tenon, so that the instrument can be broken down into an upper and a lower joint. Some wheeze will always be present, but if there is sufficient clearance between the pad and the tone hole, use a cork or other solid pad and bevel the sides to minimize the wheeze.

There is an audible "buzz" just as a key is being opened or closed but the buzz is not continuous

- The skin covering the pad has torn, most likely along the seating ring. Replace the pad.

There is a mysterious sympathetic vibration on a particular note or notes

- Often the top two trill keys vibrating against each other or against the saddle.

- Often the Ab-Eb key vibrating. Increase the tension on the spring.

- The skin from a closed pad is vibrating sympathetically.

Upper clarion (especially B-natural) "grunts" before the correct pitch comes out

- Usually this is a problem with the jaw and tongue position (see WOODWIND METHODS).

- The register key pad should lift just high enough to barely insert a nickel between instrument and pad. Too much clearance makes the "grunt" unavoidable.

- The "grunt" on these notes on some A clarinets can be helped by shortening the register tube. A technician will need to do this—it should not be shorter than .503 inch.

■ *Mechanical*

Stuck Swab

- This usually happens if there was a fold in the swab when it was inserted, and the fold gets stuck on the register key tube. If possible, pull the swab out the direction from which it came.

- If pulling a cloth swab backwards is not possible, remove the barrel and work with the upper joint alone, gently pulling alternately on one side of the cloth and then on the other and on the middle. Usually this dislodges the swab or at worst tears the swab as it is pulled through. When there is no more "give" in the swab, twisting it one direction and then the other may dislodge it from the register tube.

- Do not push the swab with a baton or stick from the top of the joint. This compresses the swab and scratches the bore.

- *Never try to work a swab out by inserting a tool through a tone hole.* A damaged tone hole is much more expensive to repair than having a technician remove a swab.

Bent bridge key (usually because of careless assembly

- Symptom: the left hand notes may all work but none of the right hand notes work. The bridge key needs to be bent back into position.

- If you do this bending yourself, the low E-flat (R1 & L1) needs to speak securely, but if the upper ("slave") pad pushes too tightly, it will not be possible to play an uninterrupted legato from low C to B or Bb. Master and slave pads must pull evenly on the cigarette paper being used to adjust the pads.

The E/B key alone will not produce a sound without putting the F key down also

- Low E and F pads misaligned. Test with a cigarette paper strip for the two keys contacting the instrument with the same amount of pressure. A scotch tape shim between the bottom of the right-hand E/B touchpiece and the crow's foot makes a good temporary repair.

- One or more of the four lower pads is not seating around its circumference. This usually happens because the player's hand was over the lower end of the lower joint rather than over the finger holes. These keys are finicky, so if you are not confident with your repair skills, it's best left to a qualified technician.

The wood tenons stick together. Cork grease does not solve problem

- This happens in more humid times of the year and to new instruments that are suddenly being played heavily. The wood in the tenons swells and wood binds against wood, creating the possibility that part of the male tenon could break off. The female portion of the tenon must be enlarged by rolling a piece of sandpaper (220 or 240) into a cylindrical shape and carefully sanding so that the cylindrical shape of the socket is preserved from top to bottom.

- As a precaution, when applying cork grease to a new instrument, rub some cork grease into the wood at the end of the tenon and even for a small distance up the inside of the bore to prevent water penetration into the wood.

E-flat Clarinet

- Sopranino clarinet intonation is particularly sensitive to mouthpiece *and barrel* design. Be sure the mouthpiece you buy tunes well on the instrument.

- The openings of the A and G# keys are particularly critical with pitch that can be raised or lowered by adjusting the thickness of their striker corks.

- The altissimo register on E-flat clarinet generally tends to be flat. In that register, E-flat clarinet players often invent a set of fingerings unlike those of the standard B-flat clarinet.

- Many professional clarinetists who play E-flat clarinet use a B-flat clarinet reed, which provides more stability and less tendency to squeak.

- All three of the major clarinet companies (Buffet, Selmer, Yamaha) make sopranino clarinets, with Buffet most commonly found in the U.S.

Bass Clarinet

- Professional model bass clarinets have an automatic double register key mechanism which compensates for the sharpness of the lowest notes and lethargy of response in the lower *clarion* register. Student bass clarinets have a single register vent, which not only renders middle-line B and some notes immediately above the break sharp, but they don't speak as well as on professional instruments.

- Most professional bass clarinetists use a set of altissimo fingerings completely unlike those of the soprano clarinet, but these fingerings only work on professional model bass clarinets with the double register vent mechanism.

- To use the same altissimo fingerings on bass (or alto) clarinet, all notes above high C# must be played with the half-hole (on the plateau extension similar to oboe for 1L).

- For most school use, bass clarinets with E-flat as the lowest note are sufficient and much less expensive than the extended instrument. However, more challenging repertoire ("Grade 6"), may necessitate the extra low notes. Recommended: Vito 7168 and Selmer 1430LP.

- Virtually all professional orchestral bass clarinetists play the extended instrument (to low C), with Buffet's 1193 Prestige and Tosca instruments (in wood or Greenline) and the Selmer Model 65 (to low Eb) and 67 (to low C) instruments dominating the market.

Reeds

(see "Understanding Clarinet and Saxophone Reeds")

Mouthpieces

- To maximize student success, upgrade from the stock plastic mouthpiece to a well-designed hard rubber one as early in a student's training as possible.

- When buying a clarinet or saxophone mouthpiece for use in classical music, look for a sound that is pleasing to the performer and listener, ease and cleanness of articulation, evenness of sound from bottom to top, *and reliable intonation* with an electronic tuner.

Recommended Brands and Facings

- Newer Vandoren mouthpieces—BD5, CL6, M30, CL5, M13, M13 lyre (in that order). Some available in Series 13, which is lower American (A440) pitch, but *test with a tuner before buying.*

- Older Vandoren mouthpieces—5RV lyre, B45, 2RV

- D'Addario Reserve

- Bass Clarinet—Vandoren B50

Understanding materials—plastic, hard rubber, crystal, or metal

- Injection-molded plastic mouthpieces are beginners' mouthpieces.

- Most quality clarinet mouthpieces, classical saxophone mouthpieces and some jazz saxophone mouthpieces are made of hard rubber. Hard rubber is easier to work and feels warmer than metal or crystal, but the facings will eventually wear out.

- Crystal (glass) feels colder and harder to the player and it is heavier than hard rubber. However, it never warps and is virtually impervious to wear on the facing.

- Metal—generally surgical steel, sometimes plated with gold—is also impervious to wear but weighs more than hard rubber. Since many jazz mouthpieces are metal, it is commonly thought that if a mouthpiece is metal it is therefore a jazz mouthpiece—however, this is not always true.

Understanding resistance and facings

- Appropriate resistance is necessary for a controllable upper register on all woodwinds. *The more open a clarinet or saxophone mouthpiece facing is, the more resistant it will be and the more closed, the less resistant. Again, the shorter a facing is, the more resistant it will be and the longer, the less resistant.* "Open" and "closed" refers to the distance between the tip of the mouthpiece and the tip of the reed, and "short" and "long" refers to the distance between the tip of the mouthpiece and the point where the facing begins to curve away from the mouthpiece's flat table.

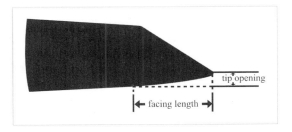

Mouthpiece facing length and tip opening

- Interior dimensions also affect resistance, but the facing remains the major variable.

Ligatures

Clarinet and Saxophone Recommendations

- Bonade (Screws under)

- Vandoren Optimum

- Rovner (Vinyl)

Points to consider

- Screw ligatures are right-handed. If the screws cannot be turned from the right with screws under the mouthpiece, the ligature is designed to be played with the screws above the mouthpiece.

- The more firmly the ligature holds the reed, the less likely the tone is to "spread." This is affected by both design and materials from which ligatures are made.

- The great question for the clarinetist is, "does this ligature hold the sound in focus at loud dynamics?"

Barrel Joints

- If a longer or shorter barrel is needed to resolve a problem of chronic flatness or sharpness staying with the brand of clarinet upon which the barrel is to be used is the safest recommendation.

- The standard length of barrel may vary from company to company— for example, the Yamaha "Custom" instrument is designed with a longer upper joint and shorter barrel, making the Buffet barrel totally incompatible with the Yamaha instrument.

- Wood barrel joints do wear out though. Try numerous new barrels and if all of them focus the sound better than the old barrel, it is time for replacement. Remember to test them with a tuner!

SAXOPHONE

Purchasing

■ *New saxophones*

- ■ Student instruments vary widely in price and quality, with the instruments at the very low end of the price range frustratingly inadequate. Always recommend that an instrument be procured from a knowledgeable music dealer.

- ■ Recommended student instruments (SATB):

    Yamaha (model 1295)

    Jupiter (model AL769, which at the time of this writing offers a warranty until the original owner graduates from high school)

- ■ Recommended Professional instruments (SATB except where indicated): While Selmer and Yamaha still dominate this market, the "gap" is closing rapidly:

    Selmer Paris, Super Action 80, Series 2 or Series 3

    Yamaha Custom and Yamaha ZZ

    Buffet Senzo (alto only)

    Keilwerth

    Cannonball

    Yanagisawa

- ■ Soprano saxophones are available in curved and straight models. In general, straight sopranos are easier to play in tune. Recommended: Selmer Series III, Yamaha Custom and Yanagasawa

Older instruments

- If buying an older instrument, avoid instruments without an articulated G# mechanism, a low B-flat key, a high F palm key or which have markings "high pitch," "low pitch," or any abbreviation "hp," "h," "lp," or "l." These instruments are obsolete.

- If an older instrument looks like a small tenor saxophone, it may be a "C Melody," which is also obsolete.

- On the other hand, an older Selmer (1954-1974) stamped "Mark VI" is the legendary professional instrument and is quite valuable.

Mouthpieces

(Always take a tuner with you when you buy mouthpieces to be sure the scale of the instrument with the chosen mouthpiece is accurate).

Classical

- Classical mouthpieces are designed for control in all ranges with reliable response and a sweeter, even, more blending sound than jazz mouthpieces. Most of these mouthpieces are hard rubber.

Alto recommendations
Vandoren Optimum AL3 and some AL4's (though these may be less consistent), and Rousseau "Classical"

Selmer S80 and Soloist Models C, C* OR D

Tenor recommendations
Vandoren Optimum TL3 AND Selmer S80 C* or D

Baritone recommendations
Vandoren Optimum B3, B4 or Selmer S80 C or C* or D

Soprano recommendations
Vandoren SL3 OR SL4 OR Selmer C, C* or D

Jazz

- Jazz mouthpieces usually have wider tip openings for greater projection and/or volume than classical mouthpieces. Even one jazz mouthpiece in a classical ensemble can create a major balance problem.

- Since there is a wide variety of jazz mouthpieces, be sure the jazz mouthpiece selected is appropriate for the intended situation. Be sure the intonation is reliable, and be sure the player can control the mouthpiece. *Do not assume that the mouthpiece is ideal or appropriate for a student because a famous jazz saxophonist plays or has played it.*

Alto recommendations
Vandoren V16 model A5, Jody Jazz (medium facing), Meyer 5 or Selmer Studio model

Tenor recommendations
Vandoren V5 Jazz Series 5 or 6, Otto Link Metal 6 , 6* or 7, Meyer hard rubber 5 or 6, or Jody Jazz hard rubber medium facing

Baritone recommendations
Vandoren Jazz Series medium facing

Soprano recommendations
Selmer D

Maintenance and Storage

- Lubrication—see Lubricants and Polishes in "Woodwinds in General"

- *Lift a saxophone by the bell—not by the narrow upper part where there are keys, rods and pads to be thrown out of adjustment by the pressure of the hand.*

- Push the neck directly down holding the tube just over the tenon— do not apply downward pressure from the cork end.

Handling saxophone by the bell and inserting neck by holding over the tenon

- Swab after playing with an appropriate saxophone swab, available from a music dealer, to keep food residue and saliva from accumulating and dripping onto the pads. Either a swab with a cord or a one-piece rigid swab (trademarks "Shove-it" or "Pad-Saver") may be used, but do not leave the moist swab inside the instrument during storage.

- Lubricate the mechanism periodically as described in "Woodwinds in General."

- The saxophone should rest securely inside the case. It may be prudent to put a small towel or chamois over or under the instrument if the case closes too easily and the instrument moves around.

- Soft "gig bags" are popular but do not adequately protect the mechanism.

- Extremes of heat should be avoided as the adhesive behind the pads becomes malleable at very high temperatures.

- Periodically, examine the saxophone with a leak light to discover any leaks that may have developed. Leaking pads should be adjusted or replaced.

Checking saxophone for leaks with a leak light

- If pads are to be replaced, be sure that the resonators on the pads are the ones designed for that particular instrument. and be sure the pads are appropriate for your instrument. (For example, do not put a Conn pad in a Selmer or Yamaha instrument or vice versa.)

Troubleshooting

For the following topics, please see "Woodwinds in General"

- Lubricants and Polishes

- Lost Motion (loose keys)

- Needle Springs Unhooked

- Needle Springs Broken

- Flat Springs Loose or Fallen Off

- Pad has fallen out

- Pad seats poorly and leaks

- Pad has split or the skin has come off

- Sticky pads

- Cork bumper has fallen off

- Basic Woodwind Toolbox

- Pads missing

- Pads leaking

- Pads sticking

- Neck cork too loose or missing

- Testing student instruments

- Rod axels or pivot screws loose

■ *Pitch*

The saxophone is generally flat or sharp

- If sharp, the neck cork may be so thin or compressed that the mouthpiece slides too far onto the neck. Have the cork replaced.

- If flat, the neck cork may be too thick and the mouthpiece will not fit far enough onto the neck. Sand the cork.

A single note is out of tune with the rest of the scale

- A pad may not be opening far enough (causing flatness) or less often, may be opening too far (causing sharpness). On many saxophones, the felt bumpers that regulate the opening distance of the very lowest pads are adjustable by turning the screw upon which they are mounted clockwise or counterclockwise. If striker corks have fallen off of palm keys, the pitch of those notes will be very sharp (and you may hear metal striking metal as the keys are opened).

Other pitch issues

- Dynamic differences affect saxophone pitch similarly to clarinet—softer is sharper and louder is flatter.

- Different saxophone mouthpieces affect intonation differently—some playing generally higher or lower, and others rendering the short fingerings (ones with few fingers down) flat to the long fingerings (ones with more fingers down).

- Fourth-line D and D# are naturally sharp on saxophones. See the Fingering Chart and Commentary sections in WOODWIND METHODS. "Dropping the jaw" is the common adjustment.

■ *Response*

Low notes do not speak or the student resorts to "Honking" in the low register

- Be sure the student is actually making an embouchure. See "WOODWIND METHODS" p. 82.

- If the embouchure is correct, there may a leak or leaks somewhere above the highest open hole, caused by a bent key, dry, shriveled or torn pad, or a bent tone hole. You can discover this with a leak light, but the repair requires a technician's expertise and tools.

- The mouthpiece may be inappropriately open for the student. Be sure the saxophonists in your classical ensemble are playing on classical mouthpieces.

- Reed is warped. See "Understanding Clarinet and Saxophone Reeds."

- The student is using a reed that is too hard for the mouthpiece and for his/her embouchure.

- If low C speaks but low C#, B and B-flat do not, the adjustment screw over the articulated G# pad is not holding the G# pad down when the C#, B and B-flat keys are depressed. Adjust with screwdriver to be sure the G# and G pads touch the instrument at the same time.

Turning the adjustment screw
on the G# key

- Dropping small object such as a cork grease tube into the bell improves the response of the lowest notes.

The low register fingerings produce upper register notes
- The octave key pad is missing or torn.
- The octave key on the neck is not seating because it has been bent in the assembly process or because the neck is incorrectly aligned..

Highest notes do not speak or they are flat
- The reed may be too soft.
- The student does not have enough mouthpiece in the mouth
- The student's jaw is not forward enough
- The octave key is not opening.

■ *Reeds*

(see "Understanding Clarinet and Saxophone Reeds")

UNDERSTANDING CLARINET AND SAXOPHONE REEDS

General Information

- The higher the number, the more resistant (i.e. "harder") the reed.

- Recommend a number 2 or 2½ for the first reeds your beginners purchase. Then adjust the strength number as you notice how the first reeds are working. (Reeds will automatically be more resistant at higher altitude also, so there is no one "perfect" recommendation).

- A reed that is too resistant (hard) will have a very fuzzy, "airy" sound and the student will tend to bite.

- A reed that is too soft will blow very easily in the lower registers, but will produce a flat pitch if it speaks at all in the upper or *clarion* register (above the "break"). So as a student's embouchure and air stream grow stronger and as the upper register becomes more necessary, the strength number can be adjusted upwards. (i.e. from no. 2 toward no. 2½, 3 or 3½).

- Do not assume that the better the player, the harder the reed. The reed must be of an appropriate strength for the player *and the mouthpiece*. Many students play reeds which are inappropriately resistant because they believe it is a mark of an advanced player.

- The resistance provided by mouthpieces varies widely. (See the mouthpiece discussion on pp. 38–39.) Some are much more resistant and others blow much more freely. Therefore, the same reed can feel hard on one mouthpiece and soft on another.

Recommended Brands

- Vandoren. Industry leader for many years. The "blue box" Vandoren is the basic product, and many other options are also offered, for example "Java Jazz" for jazz saxophone use, and V-21 and V-12 for clarinet, which is a thicker blank than "blue box."

- Rico: Reserve, Reserve Classic and Grand Concert

- D'Addario: Reserve and Reserve Classic

- Mitchell Lurie (clarinet only)

- Fred Hemke (saxophone only)

- Legere: A polymer reed which currently leads the synthetic reed market. Available for all clarinets and saxophones, this semi-transparent reed is considerably more expensive than cane reeds, but outlasts cane reeds and never warps. This is a real asset for the larger single-reed instruments—contralto and contrabass clarinet, bass saxophone—because warpage can be so extreme with a wide reed that a warped cane reed will not seal against the mouthpiece at all.

Reed Care, Break-in, Storage and Adjustment

- Plan a "break-in" period for reeds, beginning with playing a reed for just a few minutes on the first day and gradually lengthening the amount of time spent playing a reed each day.

- There are two broad categories of reed problems: organic and mechanical. If the material from which a reed is made (cane) is of inferior quality, no amount of adjusting will make it into a good reed. If the raw material is of high quality, the reed may be improved by adjustment.

- A quick way to recognize a poor piece of cane is to write on the back of the reed with a ball-point pen. The more the pen digs into the cane, the less likely it is that it will ever be a good reed, no matter how skillfully one adjusts it.

- Reed holders (cases) have two functions: (1) to prevent physical damage to the reed and (2) to control humidity and thus control reed warpage. See "Understanding Reed Warpage" below. Good reed cases are made by Vandoren, Selmer, Rico and Pro-tec, among others.

- Many reeds work better when moved to the left or to the right of the center of the mouthpiece facing. When a reed improves when pushed to the left, the right side is too resistant—correctable by gently removing some wood on the right side of the vamp of the reed with sandpaper, reed knife or Dutch rush between the beginning of the cut part and about half the distance to the tip.

(L) Sliding the reed to the left to prove that the right side is too hard
(R) Removing cane from the right shoulder to balance the reed

- Moving a reed upward on the mouthpiece increases the resistance (makes it seem "harder"), and moving it downward does the opposite.

- If the desired resistance is obtained by sliding the reed upward on the mouthpiece, a small amount of the tip may be removed with a reed clipper (for example, Cordier or Vandoren). Since clipping the tip leaves the very end thicker than before, thin the last 5 millimeters—in the center of the tip especially—with sandpaper to regain the warmth of the tone and altissimo response. A thick tip will be bright, the altissimo register will not respond well, and the reed seems to "bark" when tongued. The resistance of the reed will not be affected if only the tip is thinned.

- All other factors being equal, the wider the reed, the more difficult it is to focus the sound. Narrowing a reed slightly with sandpaper will improve the focus, but too much narrowing will make the sound "thin" or "wiry."

Correct alignment
and use of
reed clipper

- A reed will almost always sound and respond better if it has been rubbed smooth and sealed. This can be done with writing paper or the back of a sheet of sandpaper.

Understanding Reed Warpage

- Virtually all single reeds warp when wet and dried a few times, and the resistance that the player feels changes considerably when this happens.

- Warpage is usually humidity-related. Too much dryness causes (1) convex warpage, when the sides of the flat back reed pull off of a flat surface and the center stays in contact, and too much wetness causes (2) concave warpage, when the sides touch a flat surface and the center arches off the surface. Convex warpage is more common.

- To see the warpage pattern, apply a small drop of water to the back of the reed and press it against glass to see where the water is in contact and decide whether the reed is convex or concave. Regularly check the backs of single reeds and adjust the storage humidity as needed, possibly by using a more air-tight reed container or by using a sealable plastic bag with the reed holder that you have.

- It may be advisable to soak a single reed that has become convex *after* playing it to return its flatness for the next time.

- When a reed is played too much without a break-in period, the reed will warp inward toward the tip of the mouthpiece. having the effect of decreasing resistance by decreasing the distance the reed has to travel from its resting (equilibrium) position.

- Both kinds of warpage may be present in the same reed and both can be seen as the back of the reed is wet and placed on a sheet of glass.

- The tip of a reed sometimes becomes wavy, especially when it has been allowed to dry for a long time and then just barely wet again. This waviness is of little concern—soaking and playing restores the flatness to the tip.

Balance

- *In order to be balanced, the reed must work as a mirror image of the mouthpiece facing*. There is no such thing as a reed which is balanced for all mouthpieces—*balance* simply means that the resistant areas of a reed match the less resistant parts of the mouthpiece facing *in a particular player's embouchure*.

Testing for balance

- The first test to determine whether a reed is balanced or not is to roll the mouthpiece on its axis in the mouth while playing a short-tube note (like open G on clarinet or third-space C or C# on saxophone). Notice if a more colorful sound is found when pushing more on one side of the reed than the other. The side that the lip is pressing when the tone is most colorful and perhaps louder is the resistant side.

■ The second test is to try the reed moved slightly off-center one way and then the other. When the reed sounds most colorful moved to the left, the right side is too resistant, and vice versa. Removing some wood from the more resistant side of the vamp between the beginning of the cut to about halfway to the tip will balance the reed. Avoid thinning one corner of the tip or the other to balance the reed. This will only make the tone dull.

BASSOON

Purchasing

▪ *Recommended student bassoons*

- ▪ The (Fox) Renard bassoon dominates the school market. "Long Bore" and "Short Bore," options are available—"Short bore" is preferred.

- ▪ The polypropylene (black plastic) Fox bassoon is an excellent choice for durability.

- ▪ Schreiber S16—excellent choice.

- ▪ "Short Reach" brings the holes closer together for small hands—recommended for middle school

- ▪ An extended touchpiece on the wing joint for 3L is recommended for small hands, otherwise an open hole instead of a touchpiece is recommended.

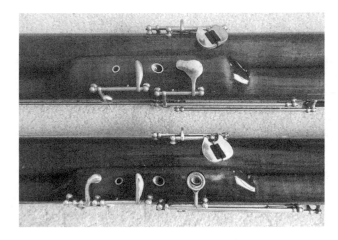

Extended touchpiece on wing joint (above),
normal configuration (below)

Step-up and professional

- At the professional level, Heckel dominates the U.S. market, with the very top Fox bassoons a close second.

Maintenance and Storage

- Always swab the bassoon after playing with an appropriate bassoon swab.

- If a swab with a cord and a weight is used, find one with a small length of the cord trailing after the cloth has gone into the instrument, so that if the swab becomes stuck in the upper joint, it may be pulled back out the wide end. (See the oboe swab pictured on page 19).

- To avoid getting the swab stuck, insert it from the small end of the wing joint.

- Drop the weighted end of the swab into the larger butt joint bore, invert and jiggle the joint until the weight comes out the other end and pull the swab through.

- Do not store the wet swab inside the instrument.

- Storage in either extremes of temperature or humidity is not recommended.

Troubleshooting

For the following topics, please see "Woodwinds in General"

- Lubricants and Polishes
- Lost Motion (loose keys)
- Needle Springs Unhooked
- Needle Springs Broken
- Flat Springs Loose or Fallen Off
- Pad has fallen out
- Pad seats poorly and leaks
- Pad has split or the skin has come off
- Sticky pads
- Cork bumper has fallen off

- Basic Woodwind Toolbox

- Pads missing

- Pads leaking

- Pads sticking

- Neck cork too loose or missing (applies to bocal cork)

- Testing student instruments

- Rod axels or pivot screws loose

- Basic Woodwind Toolbox

■ *Pitch*

Bassoon is flat or sharp overall

- Be sure the student is not taking too much reed (sharp and hollow) or too little (dull, perhaps buzzy, and flat).

- The no. 2 bocal is the standard bocal, but the specific length for a no. 2 will vary from one company to another. For example, Fox bocals are built for Fox bassoons and are shorter than those of other makers. A no. 1 bocal is shorter and will play sharper and a no. 3 is longer will play flatter than a no. 2 of the same maker.

- Temperature affects pitch. Warmer is higher and colder is flatter.

- Reed length varies. Shorter is sharper and longer is flatter.

- Softer bassoon reeds will generally play flatter than harder ones.

Individual notes are sharp or flat to the rest of the scale

- There are many fingerings available for almost every note on the bassoon, some sharper and some flatter. A fingering that works well on one bassoon might not work well on another, so choosing appropriate fingerings is vital.

- Certain problems are present on virtually all bassoons. For example, fourth-line F# and fourth-space G-natural are usually sharp. Covering more of the hole with 1L helps, and front F# is lower than back F#, but it still has to be "lipped" down.

- The interior dimension of the bocal affects pitch relationships within the scale. Before altering the bassoon itself, try other bocals.

- When a pad or striker cork of improper thickness is installed, pitch problems may occur.

- Dirt in a tone hole will make the note flat when it is the highest open hole.

- Detailed resources can be found on the internet and in Shelley Jagow's book, *Tuning for Wind Instruments: A Roadmap to Successful Intonation* (Meredith Music Publications).

The pitch sags on third space E
- Check the wire which is closest to the tip of the reed and tighten it if necessary.

- Move the top wire a little closer to the tip. If this does not solve the problem, clip a very tiny amount from the tip of the reed with a single-edged razor blade.

The B-naturals in and immediately above the staff are sharp and weak
- A cork on the low F key is missing or improperly adjusted. A repair technician issue.

■ *Response*

A, B-flat, B and C just above the bass clef do not speak (the "flick" notes)
- The hole in the dimple on the bocal is plugged. If cleaning the bocal does not open the hole, it may be necessary to use a sewing needle or a piece of wire.

Lower register is nearly impossible to play
- A pad may be missing or dislodged leaving part of a hole open. Be sure each joint holds a vacuum.

- Check for a missing, torn, or poorly seated pad.

- The reed is too hard.

- Reed may not have "lows" in the crow. When a double reed will not produce the low part of the "double crow," the lower register becomes difficult or impossible to produce.

- Test the butt joint to see if it holds a vacuum by drawing the air out of one of the two bores while holding the other against your cheek.

- The wood at the bottom of the butt joint has shrunk away from the brass fitting for the "U" tube. A repair technician can re-seal it.

Butt joint with end cap removed, showing U-tube (attached with screws), and the brass fitting between the wood and the U-tube

- Bent bocal, causing the solder seam down the length of the bocal to break open. See a qualified technician.

- Whisper key pad not covering the hole on the bocal, the pad is damaged or is missing. The whisper key pad is especially vulnerable since a careless twist of the bocal will shear the pad completely off of the key cup.

Student has difficulty playing C#/Db in and above the staff

- The keys for the left thumb out of alignment. They should all be the same height when at rest and should go down the same amount when depressed.

The reed is too hard to blow (too resistant)

- If the tip opening is large (over about ¹⁄₁₆ of an inch, gently close the reed at the first wire with pliers. If it remains too resistant, put the mandrel in the back end and the plaque or guitar pick between the blades of the reed and take a little cane off both sides with sandpaper or a reed knife. Be sure the reed is fully soaked before performing either of these procedures.

Most notes do not speak

- Leakage between the reed and the bocal. Take the reed and bocal off of the bassoon, plug the end of the bocal and the whisper key hole, suck the air out of the reed and bocal and draw it quickly out of your mouth. The reed should "pop" soon after drawing it out of your mouth.

- Bocal may have a hole in it. Replace it or have the bocal repaired.

Bocal clogged or air flow impaired

- Bocals need to be cleaned periodically. Use warm flowing water and perhaps a bocal brush. A commercial product such as CRS may be useful.

■ *Mechanical*

Broken tenon

- The male end of either tenon (but most often the wing joint) may break off as a result of not using the body lock. See a qualified technician.

Tenons too loose

- Bassoon tenons are wrapped with string. Add waxed dental floss to the male tenon to tighten the fit.

Stuck swab

- Buy swabs that have a piece of cord that follows the cloth part through the instrument so that if it does get stuck (and it will always be in the wing joint), the swab may be drawn out the large end. (The design is the same as the oboe swab pictured on page 19).

- Never try to force it the rest of the way up the narrow end as it will lodge more tightly, never try to push it with a baton or a stick, and never try to work it out through a tone hole because repairing a tone hole is more expensive than having the repair shop resolve the issue.

- To be absolutely sure this does not happen, insert the swab from the narrow end of the wing joint where the bocal is inserted.

Pad fell out

- Best to replace the pad. See "Woodwinds in General." for specific procedure.

Whisper key pad has fallen off the key cup

- Re-attach or replace with French Cement or stick shellac. This pad is lost more than any other pad on the bassoon.

Whisper key pad does not contact the bocal at the same time the pancake key (low E) contacts the butt joint

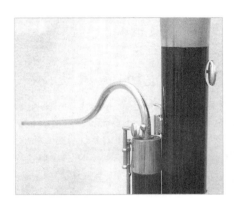

Whisper key pad and bocal with pad in open position

- Usually, this is a matter of changing the position of the wing joint with slight clockwise or counter-clockwise adjustments.

- If twisting the wing joint in the butt does not fully correct the problem, the bridge key may need a thicker cushion. A good temporary spacer is shrink tubing, found in the electrical section of a hardware store.

The pin in the body lock has broken

- These pins are meant to break rather than to cause damage to the wing or long joints so having a small supply is advisable. The silver cap is threaded, but may need to be held with pliers in order to unscrew. Slip the pin into the saddle on the long joint, put the spring over the bottom of the pin into the saddle, and screw the silver cap firmly onto the end of the pin as shown below:

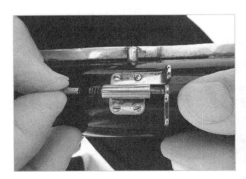

Replacing the body lock on the long joint

Bassoon Reeds

Recommended Suppliers for Bassoon Reeds

- Forrests, the Double Reed Specialists
  1849 University Ave.
  Berkeley, CA 94703 U.S.A.
  (510) 845-7178
  sales@forrestsmusic.com

- RDG Woodwinds, Inc.
  589 North Larchmont Blvd., 2nd Floor
  Los Angeles, CA 90004
  (323)463-4930

Problems with Bassoon Reeds

The reed does not fit on the end of the bocal, either causing leakage or not fitting securely

- The opening may be enlarged with a reamer specially made for bassoon reeds or with a small round file. Reamers vary—some need to be used on a dry reed; others work better with a wet reed.

- Bocals are sometimes damaged at the reed end, causing them to not be absolutely round, often as a result of careless flicking to dislodge water. A pencil or another round object may have been jammed into the end to restore the roundness causing the solder seam to rip.

The string binding ("Turk's Head" knot) has come loose or moves up or down the reed

- If the knot is only loose, usually soaking the reed long enough for the wood to swell may be all that is needed to tighten the knot. The knot may be secured with household cement such as "Duco" if needed.

- Glue from a hot melt glue gun can be spread over the lower two wires and will become strong and stable when it cools.

- Shrink tubing (found in a hardware store where electricians' supplies are located) makes an adequate substitute if the string is completely off the reed, but remember reed cane ignites easily.

The wires don't stay in place

- If the wires are loose when the reed is wet, they need to be tightened with pliers. With a mandrel in the reed, carefully lift the twisted ends of the wire, pull on them and then twist it slightly tighter. Be sure to lift the wire while twisting or it will break. (Playing without the first wire will cause the reed to play flat and be unstable on E).

Tip opening is too large or too small

- Squeezing the wire closest to the tip on the sides of the fully soaked reed with pliers perpendicular to the reed opening will open the tip. Squeezing the second wire from the tip on the sides with the pliers perpendicular to the tip will close the tip.

A "popping" sound when sustaining a note

- There is water in the lowest part of the curve in the bocal. Remove the bocal and blow the water out from the large end.

▪ *General Reed Knowledge for the Non-Bassoonist*

- Before playing, soak a bassoon reed by submerging in a glass of water for several minutes.

- All cane (organic) reeds are subject to changes of altitude, barometric pressure, humidity and weather. A reed made at low altitude will become harder at high altitude.

Soaking the entire
bassoon reed

- Simple adjustments may be made with minimal tools. Begin with a bassoon mandrel, a guitar pick or bassoon plaque, a round file, a reed knife and a pair of needle-nosed pliers. While a reamer is preferable to a round file for enlarging the bottom opening of a bassoon reed, reamers vary widely in price and the less expensive ones may be inadequate. Reed knives also vary widely in price, but a knife is more likely to be used on reeds other than bassoon, making it a wiser investment.

- If using store-bought reeds begin with a medium soft strength. Bassoon reeds must be soaked completely before playing or adjusting.

- Bassoon reeds must "crow," sounding at least two tones when blown by placing the lips past the blades onto the wires.

GLOSSARY

Adjustment Screw   A screw on a key which regulates the alignment of two pads or the rise of a pad from the instrument

Alcohol Lamp   A source of clean flame consisting of an alcohol reservoir, a wick, and a guide for the wick

Altissimo   The highest register of a woodwind instrument

Articulated G#   A G# mechanism in which the touchpiece and the key are on different axels. Closing 1R closes the G# key whether the touchpiece is down or not.

Axel (Rod Axel)   A rod running from one end to the other end of a woodwind key upon which the key pivots

Barrel Joint   The part of a clarinet between the mouthpiece and upper joint

Bladder Pad   A pad made of a cardboard ring and a felt ring, covered with a very thin, semi-transparent membrane

Bocal   The curved metal piece between the reed and the body of the bassoon or English horn itself

Bore   The hollow interior of a woodwind instrument

Bore Oil   An organic oil used to stabilize the wood of a grenadilla instrument

Bridge Key   An extension of a woodwind key that transfers motion from one joint over a tenon to another joint

Bunsen Burner   A source of clean flame using natural gas

Bushing   A plastic replacement for a tone hole seat, used after the wooden seat was compromised by a crack in the wood

Clarion   The second register on clarinet consisting of third partials

Concert Pitch   The sounding pitches on a piano or any "C" instrument

Cork Grease   Lubricant designed for cork, usually organic in origin

Cork Pad   A woodwind pad made of high-quality cork

Crown   The metal piece on the very end of the headjoint, screwed onto the flute headjoint cork assembly

Crow's Foot   The extension from the touchpiece of the F/C key on a clarinet that catches the motion of the key below it

Denatured Alcohol   The type of alcohol used in an alcohol lamp. (In contrast to isopropyl or grain alcohol)

Dutch Rush   The mildly abrasive stem of a horsetail plant used wet or dry to thin part of a reed

Facing (curve)   The curved part of the table of a woodwind mouthpiece

Flat Spring   A flat piece of metal attached to a key which causes a key to return to its original position

Flush Band   A metal band shrunk around a woodwind instrument for the purpose of holding a crack closed

French Cement   A solid adhesive which becomes malleable when heated, used to secure woodwind pads to key cups

Head Joint Face Plate   The round plate attached to a threaded screw in its center, snug against the end of a flute headjoint cork

Joint   An individual piece of a woodwind instrument, often with holes and keys

Key Cup   The part of a woodwind key in which a pad is attached, that covers a tone hole

Key Oil   A lubricant, usually petroleum-derived, used to lubricate keys on a woodwind instrument

Leak Light   A small light which is inserted in the bore of a woodwind instrument which discloses the location of leaks around the seat of the pad

Master Pad   The pad that is touched directly when a two-pad combination moves at the same time

Neck   The curved part of a saxophone between the mouthpiece and the body of the instrument (sometimes called "gooseneck")

Needle Spring   A slender piece of metal mounted between a key post and a saddle which causes a key to return to its original position

Octave Key   The key on oboes and saxophones that open a vent hole, causing the pitch to jump to a higher octave

Pad Slick   A flat piece of metal used to adjust the position of a pad while the adhesive is malleable

Pancake Key   The low E key on a bassoon butt joint

Paraffin   A petroleum derivative wax used to secure and lubricate string on bassoon tenons

Pinning   Using small pieces of threaded wire (like screws) to stabilize a crack in a woodwind instrument

Pivot Screw   A small screw at the ends of a solid key upon which the key moves freely

Plaque   A flat piece of metal used to separate the two blades of a double reed when scraping with a reed knife

Rails   The sides and tip part of a woodwind mouthpiece that touch the reed when the reed is pushed into the mouthpiece

Reamer   A tool used to remove wood from the end of a bassoon reed that attaches to the bocal

Reed well   The opening on the top of an oboe upper joint into which the reed is inserted—sometimes called *reed receiver*

Refacing   Changing the facing curve by adjusting the rails of a mouthpiece. Done with fine sandpaper

Register   All notes of a single partial, such as fundamental or first overtone

Register Key   The clarinet key operated by the left thumb that causes the instrument to produce partials above the fundamental

Resistance   The feeling that the instrument is "blowing back" at the player

Rod axel   A metal rod, threaded on one end and with a slot on the other, extending the length of a hollow metal tube part of a woodwind key

Saddle   The perturbation on a woodwind key into which the end of a needle spring is secured

Seat   A pad seats when it touches the instrument evenly around the circumference of the tone hole

Seating Ring   The ring that an instrument's seat presses into a pad

Shoulder   The area of a single reed where the bark ends and the cut part (vamp) begins

Shrink Tubing   Plastic tubing used by electricians which shrinks when heated

Slave Pad   The pad of a two-pad combination that moves when the master pad is depressed

Sopranino   An instrument of high soprano range sounding above concert pitch

Spine   An area of thicker cane running down the center of an oboe reed between the strings and the heart

Staple   The metal tube upon which an oboe or English horn reed is tied

Stock   The part of a single reed with bark on it. The ligature touches this part of the reed.

Striker   The part of a woodwind key which strikes the body of the instrument, limiting the distance the pad rises

Table   The flat part of a clarinet or saxophone mouthpiece

Tenon   The ends of a woodwind joint which attach two joints together— called "male" and "female"

Throat Tones   The seven clarinet notes from bottom-space E through B-flat

Touchpiece   The part of a woodwind key that the finger touches

Tuning Ring   A flat washer that fits between joints of a clarinet to occupy airspace caused by pulling the joint apart for tuning

Vamp   The part of a single reed from which the bark has been removed

Vent (hole)   A hole near the mouthpiece or reed, covered by a key which is opened in order to produce a higher register

Whisper Key   The bassoon key with the pad closing a hole on the bocal, used to facilitate overblowing to a higher partial

ABOUT THE AUTHOR

Recipient of the Award of Excellence, Virginia Commonwealth University School of the Arts' highest faculty honor, **Charles West** has taught all five woodwinds on the university level and has performed professionally on four of five woodwinds for more than four decades. He has been a Fulbright Scholar, President of the International Clarinet Association, and Principal or Bass Clarinetist in six professional orchestras on two continents. He holds Bachelor's degrees in Music Education and Performance from the University of Northern Colorado and the Master of Fine Arts and Doctor of Musical Arts degrees from the University of Iowa. He studied all five woodwinds with Loren Bartlett, with further flute study with Watler Smith, Keith Pettway and Evelyn Tyrell, oboe study with James Lakin, clarinet study with Himie Voxman, Robert Marcellus and Leon Russianoff among others, and bassoon study with Ronald Tyree.

West has held professorships in three North American universities and guest professorships or residencies in South America, Taiwan, Hong Kong, Australia and China. He has recorded repertoire on the Klavier, Wilson Audiophile, Centaur, CRI and Crystal labels and on a Grammy Award-winning Telarc CD and has played flute, piccolo, oboe, English Horn, clarinet, bass clarinet, and all saxophones as a first call doubler in Richmond, Virginia and El Paso, Texas. He served for twenty-eight years as Coordinator of Winds & Percussion at Virginia Commonwealth University, is artist-clinician for the Buffet Crampon Group, and Conductor of the Youth Orchestra of Central Virginia. He keeps an active schedule as a public school clinician and adjudicator, and lectures and publishes internationally about reed-making and adjustment, clarinet, and general woodwind topics. His previous publications with Meredith Music Publications are *The Woodwind Player's Cookbook: Creative Recipes for a Successful Performance* (2008), and *WOODWIND METHODS: An Essential Resource for Educators, Conductors and Students* (2015).